A CENTURY *of*
THE NORTH WALES COAST

GREETINGS FROM
LLANDUDNO

THE PIER AND LITTLE ORMES HEAD FROM HAPPY VALLEY

LLANDUDNO BA

ESPLANADE AND GREAT ORMES HEAD

WEST SHORE BEACH AND GREAT ORMES HEA

The suspension bridge over the River Conwy at Conwy, taken from the castle, *c.* 1950.

A CENTURY *of* THE NORTH WALES COAST

CLIFF HAYES

WHSmith

First published in the United Kingdom in 2002 by
Sutton Publishing Limited exclusively for
WHSmith, Greenbridge Road, Swindon SN3 3LD

British Library Cataloguing in Publication Data
A catalogue record for this book is available from the British Library.

ISBN 0-7509-3083-7

Illustrations

Front endpaper: Children and adults thrill to Professor Codman's Punch and Judy show on Llandudno front, *c.* 1900.
Back endpaper: A busy Church Walks, Llandudno, 1970s.
Half title page: A general postcard of Llandudno issued in the 1960s.
Title page: A clever postcard that dates from 1913 with the words North Wales made out of scenes from the area.

Typeset in 11/14pt Photina and produced by
Sutton Publishing Limited, Phoenix Mill,
Thrupp, Stroud, Gloucestershire GL5 2BU.
Printed and bound in England by
J.H. Haynes & Co. Ltd, Sparkford.

This book is dedicated to the late William 'Scotty' Patterson who for many years ran bookshops in Llandudno and stood on Abergele market every Sunday come rain or shine.

Looking down on Llandudno and Happy Valley from the top of the Great Orme in the mid-1950s.

Contents

King George V and Queen Mary flank their son Prince Edward at his investiture as Prince of Wales at Caernarfon Castle in July 1911. This title is historically bestowed upon the eldest son of the royal family on his coming of age.

Introduction

Wales is roughly 60 miles wide and 200 miles deep. Just as Yorkshire has split into three Ridings with natural ease, Wales has divided into three main areas with rivers and mountains marking the boundaries: South Wales, Mid Wales and North Wales. Each of these areas is equally fascinating and in striking contrast to the others, from the high mountains of Snowdonia to the rolling valleys of South Wales, and the rugged coastline of Pembrokeshire to the wide sandy beaches in the north. The area most people call North Wales roughly starts at Queensferry and runs down to Harlech (including Anglesey). This part of Wales, with its flat coastal strip, has always been easily accessible to the people of northern England. When the River Dee silted up in about 1600, it was Holyhead, on Anglesey, that took a lot of shipping traffic to Ireland and the coast road into North Wales became important.

Man has lived in North Wales since the earliest times. There are caves in the Gwlyd Valley where the bones of wolves and bears have been found, together with other signs that primitive man once dwelled there. The pre-Celtic tribes, sometimes referred to as Iberians, came from southern Spain and Portugal to the area around the Irish Sea. The Celtic people reached Wales about 2,000 years ago. By the time the Romans arrived in the area the Celts had been pushed back into the hills and were contained in what we now call North Wales.

The Romans came to Wales in about AD 50 and with much trepidation, as they had heard stories about the wild, fierce local tribes, but they were keen to gain access to the rich mineral deposits found there. They sailed along the coastline and up the River Dee to establish lead mines at Holywell and copper mines at the Great Orme; they also found silver on Anglesey. They established Deva – Chester – and it is thought that they set up camps at Prestatyn and on the Great Orme. Of course they met with strong resistance from the local Druids and there were many battles. In AD 61 thousands of Druids and their followers were slaughtered on Anglesey; this greatly reduced their influence in North Wales and forced them to flee to more remote areas. The Romans continued to mine on the island, but the fact that it was an island made it necessary to build and maintain flat-bottomed boats to transport men and materials across the Menai Strait. This difficulty eventually led to the Romans abandoning their excavations there. As the Roman influence waned, the Irish raiders plucked up courage and attacked the coast, and many hill forts were constructed to repel them.

From 400 the Celtic holy men who brought Christianity to Wales came to the fore. 'Llan' is the Celtic word for church and many places were named after the churches founded there. Dewi (David), Tudno, Beuno, Eilo and Padarn all established religious centres at this time. The construction of Offa's Dyke was begun in about 784 by King Offa, the Christian ruler of the kingdom of Mercia. It reached from Flintshire to South Wales and marked the battle lines between the Saxons and the Celtic Welsh in the ninth century.

The High Street, Holywell, *c.* 1950. Holywell takes its name from the Holy Well of St Winifred that is situated here. Holywell stands on the side of Halkyn Mountain and was at one time known as Treffynnon. In the mid-twentieth century about 6,000 people lived at Holywell and worked in the woollen mills, paper mills and lead mines in the town.

It is said that the early English tribes living in the south Lancashire and Cheshire areas moved into North Wales just after the Romans left British shores in the early fifth century. This may have been to get away from the Norse and Viking raiders who were invading via Yorkshire at this time. It was Edward I (1272–1307) who decided that it was necessary to subdue and conquer the Welsh people, and to do this he required a string of castles and a heavy hand. Edward I knew his enemy well and planned for dual access to all his castles by land and sea. After a day's march from Chester he set up camp and dug in. He had stockpiled timber and an army of diggers at Chester and within hours they had started on the fortifications. Wood was floated down the Mersey on rafts from his brother's estate at Toxteth and from his own estates in Cheshire. This meant that reinforcements could reach the castles from the Irish Sea if under siege. Even inland at Rhuddlan you can see where hundreds of diggers had deepened and canalised the River Clwyd to bring ships right up to the castle walls for this purpose. The fortification at Flint became his foothold in North Wales – his 'flint-head', his spear against the Welsh, and perhaps this is how the town acquired its name.

Today one of the delights for both tourists and locals is to visit one of the great castles of North Wales. Conwy Castle, Caernarfon and Harlech are still very impressive edifices and there are smaller but charming castles at Beaumaris, Rhuddlan and Denbigh. Flint Castle is another, although mainly forgotten, gem of North Wales history. All these were built by Edward I in his efforts to subdue the Welsh people. He had been overlord of Chester since being handed the land and castles by his father King Henry III in 1254. Many of the castles he inherited were motte-and-bailey (wooden) fortifications but he held on to the area and built huge stone edifices in their place. Edward was pitted against Llywelyn ap Gruffydd (the last), who was the greatest Prince of Wales in the true sense of the word. He was a Welsh aristocrat who fought hard to carve out a kingdom in North Wales. In 1258 all lords swore allegiance to him and it seems he ruled very fairly. In 1260 he took the side of the English barons who were opposed to Henry III and in 1267 Henry grudgingly made peace with him under the Treaty of Montgomery.

The situation changed dramatically with the death of Henry III in 1272. As soon as Edward I returned from the Crusades his battles with Llywelyn began. The Welsh prince would not swear fealty to Edward and failed to attend the king's coronation in 1274. He also refused to answer five summonses between December 1274 and 1276 and so it was inevitable they would come to blows. In August 1275 Edward I had tried to make peace with Llywelyn at Chester, but again the prince did not appear. In November 1276 Edward's patience snapped. He raised a military force of unprecedented numbers and in June 1277 set off from Chester Castle to sort out this 'Rebel and Disturber of the Peace' once and for all. Edward was later to go down in history as 'the Hammer of the Scots', but Edward was also the monarch who laid down the formula for North Wales for the next thousand years.

The greatest turning point was when the House of Tudor came to the throne of England in the person of Henry VII. The Welsh now had their own man as king and they supported him wholeheartedly, looking to London as their capital and regarding the English as more or less their fellow subjects. This goes some way to explain Welsh involvement in the Wars of the Roses and the support they gave Charles I during the Civil War.

The introduction of the railways in the 1850s opened up the North Wales coast. The beautiful scenery, the fresh air and invigorating environment made this an ideal place to escape the drab and smoky cities of the industrial revolution, and many wealthy people did just that. They took holidays and even built their own homes along this beautiful coastline. By 1900 and the introduction of paid working holidays, thousands flocked to North Wales for a break. Resorts boomed, bringing new wealth and a new industry – tourism.

The Queen's Palace Hotel, Rhyl, and the Variety Theatre on the front, c. 1903. The amusement centre with its fabulous roof garden opened in 1902 and offered an unbelievable range of entertainment. It had an Ashanti village where you could wander through part of West Africa and also a waxworks. The ballroom was said to be the biggest in Great Britain at the time, accommodating 2,000 couples on the sprung dance floor. There was an underground canal and an electric lift to take you to the top of the tower to view the Isle of Man. In addition there were monkeys and the 'wild man of Borneo'. It was a great shame that it burnt down in November 1907 and was never replaced.

The Main Characters in the History of North Wales

Llywelyn the Great, Llywelyn ab Iorwerth, 1173–1240

Llywelyn was born at Dolwyddelan, where his father was ruler of the area. The young prince spent many years in England till his father died and was crowned Prince of Gwynedd in 1194 at the age of twenty-one. He married King John's illegitimate daughter Joan, which meant he was interested in the fortunes of both Wales and England. His uncles took control of the area but it became fragmented and there was fighting between Anglesey and West Gwynedd. Llywelyn's strong personality and impressive leadership skills brought all these disparate elements together, and by 1210 he had been titled and crowned Prince of Wales.

Llywelyn the Last, Llywelyn ap Gruffydd, 1247–82

Llywelyn was ruler of West Gwynedd by 1246, and after his brother died he gained control over Gwynedd (1247). From 1258 he was styled Prince of Wales. Llywelyn was the last Welsh person actually to control North and Central Wales.

Edward I, 1239–1307 (ruled from 1272)

Edward married Eleanor, sister of the King of Spain, when he was only fourteen years old. He led the fight against Simon de Montfort from 1264 to 1267. Edward's campaign against the Welsh began in 1282. As a result he spent a five-year period either at Chester or in North Wales, mostly at Rhuddlan.

Owain Glyn Dwy, Owen Glendower, c. 1359–1415

Owen led the Welsh resistance that started in about 1400 and culminated in the defeat of Henry IV. He was not of royal blood but a teacher and a natural organiser. Owen was the last Welsh national to claim the title Prince of Wales. Little is known about his early life, but he became the voice of the Welsh in their complaints of ill-treatment at the hands of their English overlords. Owen's rebellious acts encouraged others across Wales and he captured Conwy Castle in April 1401. His daughter married Edmund Mortimer, an English leader, who was seized and then converted to the Welsh cause.

Master James of St George, c. 1250–1308

James was born at St George in France. He was brought to North Wales to design and oversee the building of Edward I's castles. He was a master mason and was in charge of every single detail of the construction. It was an important job and the pay was high, 2s per day and a promised pension of 3s, which he received from 1284. Master James went with Edward to Scotland and built twelve castles there. He retired to Mostyn, North Wales, and the villages built around his house took the name St George. Records indicate that Master James was the highest paid man of his time.

The Castles of North Wales

The walls of the castle at Denbigh, mid-1920s. This imposing castle, which looks out over the Vale of Clwyd with the town nestling beneath it, has had a very chequered history. It was first built as a small wooden hill fortress by the Welsh. When Edward I conquered Wales he gave it to the Earl of Lincoln. He replaced the stronghold with a magnificent castle. After the death of the Earl of Lincoln, the castle became the possession of a number of courtiers, including Hugh de Spencer, one of the unworthy favourites of Edward II. Charles I took refuge here after his retreat from Chester in 1645, and it was the last Welsh fortress to hold out for him, after a siege lasting nearly nine months. It was then dismantled and after the Restoration Charles II ordered that it be blown up. The outline of the castle is still marked by walls and towers. On the edge of the castle is Leicester's Folly, the ruins of a cathedral planned by the Earl of Leicester to replace the cathedral at St Asaph and which was never completed.

Ewloe Castle, built by the Welsh prince Llywelyn ap Gruffudd in about 1257 to help keep out the English. Though it is now surrounded by trees, at the time of its construction it would have afforded magnificent views over the border lands and even as far as the English stronghold of Chester. This castle was completed and defended the border before the time of Edward I. After a bloody battle it fell into English hands and much of it was taken down. Today it is not very accessible and is approached across a field.

Five of Edward I's North Wales castles, seen here on a postcard printed in Holland in the 1950s. Clockwise from top left the are Conwy, Rhudlan, Harlech, Caernarfon and Flint.

Hawarden Castle, 1902.

The gateway to Hawarden Castle, 1990s. This stronghold is situated on private land owned by the Gladstone family but can be visited during the summer.

There is not much left of the original castle at Hawarden, but here the huge circular keep is seen, 2002. Part of the Banqueting Hall is also still standing.

Main picture: Conwy Castle and the bridges over the River Conwy, 1920. Conwy is reputed to be Europe's most perfectly preserved medieval walled town, and is certainly very picturesque, set between the broad Conwy estuary and the foothills of Snowdonia.

Above: Flint Castle on the River Dee, 2001. Every year thousands of visitors drive along the North Wales coast road from Queensferry to Prestatyn and pass through Flint without realising that the town has a unique castle. The first of Edward's castles, it was built with the inner defences outside the main walls. This meant you had to storm the fortress and then fight your way back out over a very narrow bridge to the final defences. So few people visited the castle that a few years ago they took away the toll booth and fences and made it free and open to all.

Harlech Castle, built as much to overawe and subdue as to fortify the area. The scene below shows the castle dominating the town and looking out over the Irish Sea. The flat area to the left is said to have been the site of many battles and the burial place of thousands of warriors.

Caernarfon Castle looking across the harbour at the mouth of the River Seiont, as seen on a Valentine's postcard dating from the early 1950s. Caernarfon, which was once the British fortress Caer Seiont and the Roman military station Segontium, is situated in a most beautiful position with the wild, rugged mountains of Snowdonia behind it.

The lovely broad walk that runs alongside Caernarfon Castle in a view from 1911.

An artist's impression of Caernarfon Castle, and a lady in Welsh costume, c. 1900. These type of postcards were very popular in Edwardian times.

Gwyrch Castle at Abergele. This castle dominates the hillside as you travel down the A55, and looks for all the world like another beautiful and ancient Welsh castle. In fact it is a mock castle begun in 1819 by the Bamford Hesketh family of Rufford as a wedding present for Mr Lloyd Hesketh Bamford Hesketh and his new bride. Mr Lloyd's maternal family were the Lloyds of Gwyrch (meaning place of the hedge) and this gave the castle its name. It passed through various branches of the family, finally becoming the home of the Earl of Dundonald. The castle is 500 ft long and has eighteen embattled towers; the tallest is the Hesketh Tower which is 93 ft high.

Although at the moment Gwrych Castle is not open to the public, it has long been the subject of controversy concerning its ownership and use. During the Second World War it came under Army control and after this it was converted to an entertainment centre. Owned by Leslie Salts, it became the venue for exhibition fights between world boxing champion Randolph Turpin and his brother Dick. Later it was used as a retreat and Christian centre and in the late 1980s was occupied by hippies and squatters.

Penrhyn Castle, near Bangor, 1930. This was one of several homes built to resemble the castles found all the way down this coast. The Pennant family owned the area and they had made their money from the slate mines and quarries on their land. Survey work started in about 1827 and building in about 1830. In 1837, the year that Queen Victoria came to the throne, the outside of the house was completed and the great stained-glass windows were put into place. The house and its 40,000 acres of land were conveyed to the National Trust in 1951.

Bodelwyddan Castle, c. 1920. The house we see today was started by Sir John Williams in about 1805 and its rebuilding and growth continued until at least 1870. During the First World War it was used as an officers' mess and recuperation hospital for the Army. In 1918 Sir William Willoughby Williams (a ne'er-do-well) sold off the land of the estate, and after the Army moved out in 1920 the hall operated as a school in various forms and names until 1982. After a few years standing empty Clywd County Council bought Bodelwyddan and in a joint effort with the National Portrait Gallery established the Welsh National Portrait Gallery. Lack of funds forced the council to sell off part of the building as a hotel but the two concerns seem to run well side by side.

Bodlondeb Castle, Llandudno, 1949. Even some private houses built during the last century acquired the grand title 'castle' and Bodlondeb is one of the most interesting of these. It is now one of the leading hotels in Llandudno. It is rumoured that Edward, Prince of Wales, the future Edward VII, used to stay (privately) at the St George's Hotel in Llandudno, where it is said he entertained a young lady called Lily Grant in his suite. He mentioned to the hotel manager that if a private house was built nearby and looked after by the hotel he would pay for everything, but anonymously. So in 1898 Bodlondeb Castle was built and the lady moved in. The Prince visited quite often but the lady apparently did not like the house because 'people could see her from the road, when she was in the garden'. When Edward became king the house was given up and rented out to a family. At the back of the property was another building that started life as a Methodist church and then became a church school. It proved too small for the number of children wanting to attend and when Bodlondeb was turned into a hotel these buildings became part of the new business. Note the crown on the tower, perhaps a connection with Edward. The hotel can be found on Church Walks, Llandudno, right next to the Great Orme tramway station.

St Winifred,
St Margaret & St Asaph

The Holy Well of St Winifred, *c.* 1920. History and local folklore tell us that Winifred was a sweet young maiden, who lived with her parents in Halkyn, the early name for Holywell. The villain of the piece was Caradoc, a Welsh prince who lived in the area. Winifred refused to marry him, so he attempted to carry her off by force. She fled, pursued by Caradoc who in his rage struck off her head, which bounded down the hill to the church and on the spot where it rested a spring burst forth. Winifred's uncle, St Beuno, who was officiating in the church at the time, replaced the severed head and in answer to his prayers it was reunited with the body and the young girl was restored to life. Winifred became a nun and ended life, fifteen years later, as abbess of a convent at Gwytherin near Llanrwst. Her body was eventually moved to Holywell. Henry VIII ordered the destruction of her shrine and today just one of her fingers remains and is brought out on special occasions. The land here, including the well, is owned by the Duke of Westminster. It was leased to Holywell Council, who in turn have leased it, since 1873, to the Roman Catholic community of Holywell. Many generations of people have credited the well with miraculous virtues and pilgrims from all parts of the world come to bathe in the waters.

A London and North Western Railway bus from Holywell station at the bottom of the hill on the main railway line up to the well itself, 1906. At one time the most active spring in Great Britain, the Holy Well of St Winifrid once produced between 2,400 to 3,000 gallons per minute. Because the flow was cut off by mining operations in 1917 today it is just over 1,000 gallons per minute. Being on a hill, the well always posed parking problems and the driver of this bus is obviously not certain of his brakes. He has parked across the road.

Looking from Holywell down the Greenfield valley to the estuary of the River Dee at the bottom. As the water from the well travelled along the valley it powered many mills, including a paper mill, a pin mill and a brewery.

St Margaret's Church, Bodelwyddan, known as the Marble Church. The exterior is locally quarried limestone but the inside is decorated with some of the finest marble inlays in Wales – Belgian red marble, Irish black marble and Scottish marble are all to be found in the choir. The church was started in 1880 by the Dowager Lady Margaret de Broke of the Williams family who lived at Bodelwyddan Castle across the road. She built it in honour and remembrance of her late husband the 16th Baron Willoughby de Broke. There was a local joke that she was a Williams when building started but having spent £60,000 by the time it was completed she was 'de Broke'. It is said to be the most photographed parish church in Wales and with its 202-ft spire it is certainly very striking.

The beautiful font in St Margaret's church. It was made by Peter Hollins and fashioned out of white Carras marble. The figures depicted are of two young girls, the daughters of Sir Hugh Williams, brother of Lady Margaret, and it is said they are a good likeness. Mary Charlotte Lucy holds the shell while the younger Arabella Antonia stands behind her. Both ladies lived long lives and now rest in the churchyard. The church contains many other interesting items including a fine pulpit and a lectern, which are said to be some of the finest examples of English wood carving from the 1800s.

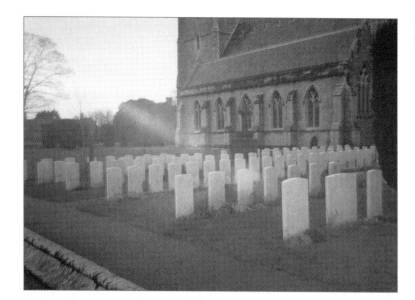

St Margaret's Church today, showing the war graves.

There are 117 war graves, 83 Canadian and 34 British. Kinmel Camp is in the parish and it was here that Canadian soldiers waiting to return home after the First World War were based. Promises made to workers during the war were not kept, many groups were on strike and ships and fuel were not available. Twice the soldiers were taken to Liverpool ready for the journey home and twice they were brought back to North Wales. These men were not being paid either. Then fate dealt them a deadly blow when Britain was hit by influenza; this took more lives than the war itself. On the night of 5 March 1919, the soldiers rioted and tried to break into camp shops for food and drink. Some of them had German guns that they had kept as souvenirs. As a result, four of the soldiers were killed and a stray bullet shot one of the guards. These five, now forgiven and resting in peace, joined the other seventy-nine Canadians in the graveyard, and every Armistice Day the graves are visited by soldiers from the Canadian Army and flowers and wreaths are laid.

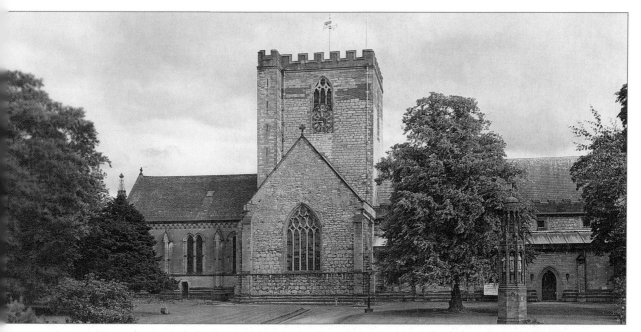

The cathedral at St Asaph, 1950. St Asaph is a city, though probably the smallest in Great Britain, and the cathedral is certainly one of the smallest in Wales. The church was established in about 550 when St Kentigern (nicknamed St Mungo – the Beloved) fled from Strathclyde to escape invaders and settled in a small protected area nestling between the rivers Clwyd and Elwy in North Wales. When Mungo thought it safe to return north, he left Asaph, his second-in-command, in charge and Asaph built up a monastery and a large wooden church here. Nothing remains of that early church as it was burnt down by Edward I in 1245.

St Asaph's Cathedral with the Bishop William Morgan monument on the left, c. 1920. The north side of the church, seen here, is now the main entrance, but this was originally the west door which is located to the right. In 1588 Bishop Morgan produced the first complete Bible in the Welsh language. Before him William Salesbury had produced a New Testament and a Book of Common Prayer. These men are featured on the monument and are dressed in their doublet and hose, which was unusual at the time. The monument was erected in 1888 with money from public subscription and has been well preserved over the years.

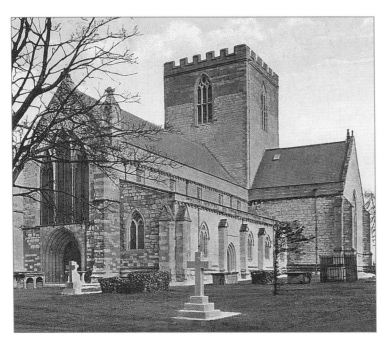

St Asaph's Cathedral viewed from the Dean's House, 1907. On the tower you can clearly see the repairs made in darker stone after Owen Glendower set fire to the church in 1402. It lay in ruins for eighty years until restored under Bishop Redman. The area behind the cathedral is the parish graveyard and while some of the bishops lie here, the most interesting grave is the one with railings round it, the grave of Dick of Aberdaron (Richard Robert Jones). He was a learned man who could speak about fifteen languages, but who preferred to wander as a tramp. He wrote a Welsh–Hebrew–Greek dictionary but could not raise the money to get it printed. The original manuscript is still housed in the church library.

The choir and altar at the east end of the cathedral in 1919. Much of the church was rebuilt under Sir Gilbert Scott between 1870 and 1880, but the stalls date from about 1260 and the time of Bishop Anian II. The canopied chair at the far end, to the right of the picture, is the bishop's seat; in the Lady Chapel on the right is an ivory Madonna from the 1500s, which is said to have been found on one of the sailors washed up on the beach after a galleon belonging to the Spanish Armada was wrecked near Pensarn. There are memorials to the Brown family whose daughter Felicia Hemans (née Brown) was a prolific poet; her work included 'Casabianca', with the immortal first line 'The Boy Stood on the Burning Deck'.

Prestatyn

Prestatyn and some lucky Welsh heather, 1950. Prestatyn is the first of the holiday towns that most visitors encounter when coming into Wales from Liverpool, Manchester and the north. A hundred years ago it was the first stop for the London & Midland fast trains bringing holiday-makers to Wales. The name Prestatyn is a mixture of English and Welsh and means 'the place of the priest'. The town is a very strange mixture of old and new and the area has been inhabited since the Stone Age. In the eighteenth century the area was sparsely populated and mainly featured fishermen's cottages and a few large farmhouses.

The bottom end of Prestatyn High Street, *c.* 1920.

Looking up Prestatyn High Street from the very bottom by the railway station, early 1920s. The population of the town double
during the decade 1911–21 and at the time of this photograph Prestatyn was fast becoming a popular holiday destination. Th
sea front offered many attractions – an open-air swimming pool, with flood-lit bathing at night, concerts and dancing in th
Pavilion and plenty of cafés and shelters. Behind the modern little town the land spread out to the hills, culminating i
Newmarket Cop (805 ft above sea level).

Prestatyn High Street, c. 1930. This thriving little town attracted hundreds of families from Liverpool, Chester and Manchester to settle here, as well as the thousands who came here for their holiday, testament to its charm and picturesque surroundings. Many of the buildings seen here are still recognisable today. Prestatyn once had a castle and just a little of its foundations can still be seen in Marine Road just behind the Nant Hall Hotel.

An early photograph of the front at Prestatyn, c. 1903. This area, before Pochin developed it, had been used by the Revd Frank Jewel and his son to grow asparagus, which they did very successfully. At the spring high tides this area and the Warren would flood and drown rabbits living there, which were then collected and sold in the local markets. The quite substantial building seen here was the café and stood where the Nova swimming pool and bar complex is today. Prestatyn has always enjoyed a good reputation for the lovely walking country around the town.

Beach Road, Prestatyn. This late Victorian photograph shows how hard it must have been pushing bassinets (prams) an wheel-chairs down the unmade sandy road to the sea. Today the road is known as Bastion Road. An early advertising sloga described the town as having 'Air like honey and low rainfall'.

The steep road that runs along the side of the Cross Foxes at the top of the High Street, Prestatyn, *c.* 1947. The hill is 805 high and is called Balloon Hill or Newmarket Cop on old maps. The Cross Foxes was once a large house called Ty Mawr an in 1808 a travel writer, Mrs Thrale, a friend of Dr Samuel Johnson, stayed there and wrote a poem about how healthy th area was. You can just make out the balustrades of the viewing points in the hillside gardens.

he garden and look-out point half-way up Ffordd Las, 1920s. High up on Ffordd Las the council laid out gardens and iewing points in Mount Ida Road, where walkers could stop and admire the spectacular views of Prestatyn and the irrounding area. These hillside gardens were very popular with holiday-makers staying in the area. From these resting oints you could also watch the ocean liners way out at sea heading either in or out of the port of Liverpool.

ant Hall, part of the Nant estate bought by Henry Davis Pochin, ex-mayor of Salford, in the late 1870s. It is currently a otel and has been for the last 60 years – I have had some good Sunday lunches here. This is how it looked in 2002.

35

The open-air bathing pool on the front at Prestatyn, mid-1950s. The reclaimed land meant there was plenty of space for leisure development. Although no longer there, this pool boasted flood-lit bathing at night and the adjoining pavilion (top left) held concerts and dances.

Prestatyn Holiday Camp, c. 1946. The lovely unspoilt area around Prestatyn attracted many people from Manchester and Liverpool, as it was easily accessible by train or road. Many came for camping or caravan holidays. Several holiday camps sprang up and Pontins is still busy in summer and winter. Two camps that had been established earlier and no longer exist were the Prestatyn Holiday Camp and the Salford Poor Children's Camp, which were run by Salford Council. This allowed impoverished children from the city slums to enjoy the seaside and was also a healthy treat, which hundreds of children had the opportunity of experiencing.

Rhyl

.. Price Twopence ..

— NEW —

HANDBOOK AND GUIDE

TO

RHYL

AND ITS VICINITY.

Photo.]   *THE PIER & PAVILION, RHYL.*   [*Bedford.*]

AND THE WALKS, DRIVES AND EXCURSIONS

IN THE NEIGHBOURHOOD.

WITH A TIME TABLE.

BY EDGAR BROOKS.

Printed and Published by ...

J. b. Allday, Shakespeare Press, Edmund St., Birmingham.

The title page of a *Handbook of Rhyl, c.* 1900. The photograph shows the old pier pavilion that burnt down in 1901. Prospective visitors sent 3*d* to the town clerk's department for the booklet and spent the winter months planning their week's holiday. In 1825 the population of Rhyl was under 1,000 and the main occupations were fishing and looking after the growing number of visitors. The situation changed dramatically in the mid-nineteenth century with the arrival of the railway. This opened up the North Wales coast to the masses and soon Rhyl became known as the 'playground of the North Wales coast'. By 1850 there were over 600 houses and hotels in Rhyl and the population had risen to over 4,000. Rhyl became an individual parish and Holy Trinity Church, built in 1835 as a Chapel of Ease, became the parish church, breaking away from St Mary's, Rhuddlan. In 1852 town commissioners were appointed and they ran Rhyl until 1894 when Rhyl Urban District Council was created. In the years between the First and Second World Wars, Rhyl became a favourite resort with up to 100,000 visitors in the course of each season. Its magnificent beaches, long promenade and pier all added to Rhyl's many attractions.

The open-air roller-skating rink on the front at Rhyl. The beach is full with families content just to get away – mother fussing, father having a bet or slipping away for a quiet pint and youngsters building sandcastles.

The pavilion at Rhyl and children paddling on the sands, 1912. The new pavilion, as it was referred to at the time, had opened on 30 July 1908 on the site of an earlier more elaborate building, which had opened in 1891 but been destroyed by fire in 1901. The pavilion seen here was pulled down in 1974.

Rhyl now has a Sea Life Centre, an excellent attraction for the resort.

he sands at Rhyl, 1920s. Note the number of very distinctive wicker chairs on the beach, which provided a seat and shelter
om the sun and wind all in one. You can even see four of them put together to form a changing room in the foreground.

he sands at Rhyl and the Pavilion Theatre viewed from Rhyl pier, early 1950s. Rhyl pier was built in 1867 at a cost of
23,000 and was a marvel of Victorian ironwork. It finally closed in 1966 and was taken down in March 1973 after years
trying to raise money to save it.

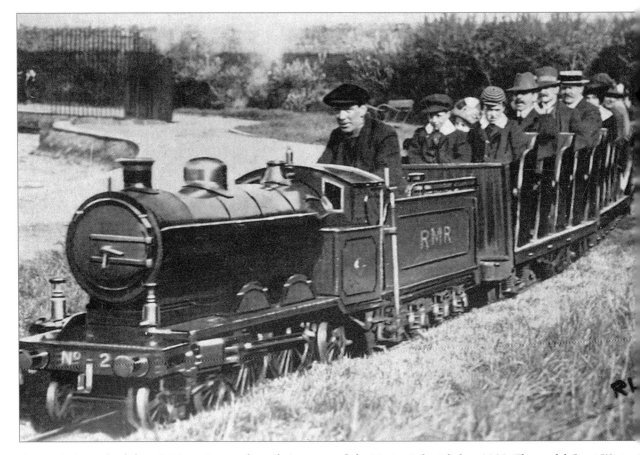

A rare photograph of the miniature steam railway that ran round the Marine Lake, Rhyl, *c.* 1920. The model Great Wester train seems to be handling her full load, including adults, with ease. The Marine Lake opened on Queen Victoria's birthda (24 May) in 1895 and was built at a cost of £10,000. The railway was built in 1911 by Miniature Railways Limited in 15- sections of 15-in gauge track. The first engine, called *Prince Edward of Wales*, was built by the Basset Lowke Company. B 1912 the railway had been taken over by Rhyl Amusements Limited. There were six four-wheeled coaches that could eac seat sixteen passengers.

An advertisement for the Palace Hotel from a 1930s guidebook.

Wellington Road, Rhyl, viewed from the corner of High Street, *c.* 1908. The town hall clock and tower stand out on this Edwardian photograph. Although the area around Rhyl is very flat, the name Rhyl has developed from a strong Welsh and English mixture: 'yr' (Welsh) and 'Lyll' (Old English): both mean the hill. Yrhyll is how the name was first recorded and this had evolved to Ryhull by about 1350. The land does slope downwards towards Old Colwyn and towards St Asaph, so it could come from that. Rhyl first attracted visitors, mainly artists and writers, during the Regency and Georgian periods. They came for inspiration and would stay in farmhouses and cottages to take in the fresh air and eat plenty of good fresh vegetables and Welsh mutton.

Bath Street, Rhyl, *c.* 1908. St Thomas's Church is on the left. The foundation stone of the church was laid in 1861 by Sir Watkins Williams Wynn and Mrs Rowley of Bodelwyddan. Built at a cost of £13,000, the church was opened in 1862 and consecrated in 1869. Later additions to the church were designed by Sir Gilbert Scott and cost twice as much as the original church itself. The reredos was given by Mr and Mrs Bamford-Hesketh of Gwrych Castle. Jack Hylton, the famous band leader, was married here.

The mouth of the River Clwyd, which has always provided a safe, natural harbour at Rhyl, with Kinmel Bay on the far bank *c.* 1900. The Voryd is the name given to the mouth of the river here. The original landing stage for Rhyl is behind the masted ship on the right. Sunny Rhyl grew where it is because of the River Clywd, the mouth of which offered shelter for fishermen. The tide provided the river mouth with a place for unloading and loading cargoes, including vegetables, corn, timber, fish and meat for the markets of the larger towns along the coast.

An interesting photograph of the Voryd (Rhyl harbour), *c.* 1907. The steam tug based in the harbour is pulling a three masted ship out to open water while holiday-makers look on.

The new Foryd Bridge, Rhyl, 1933. This bridge, which is still in use today, opened on 18 June 1932 at a cost of £66,000. Before it was built here had been a stone toll bridge here dating from 1860 and before that just a ford across the river at low tide. In 1923 the new coast road from Prestatyn into Rhyl opened and this necessitated a better crossing here.

Rhyl

Queen's : *R.* and *b.*, 9/- ; *l.*, 3/6 *t.*, 1/6 ; *d.*, 5/-.
Boarding terms : 15/6 per day.

Imperial.

Pier : *R.* and *b.*, 8/6 ; *l.*, 3/- ; *t.*, 1/6 ; *d.*, 4/-.
Boarding terms : fr. 12/6 per day.

Palace.

Westminster : *R.* and *b.*, fr. 9/6 ; *l.*, 3/6 ; *t.*, 1/6 ; *d.*, 5/6. . .
Boarding terms : fr. 15/- per day.

Grosvenor, Bodfor Street.

Marlborough (*private*), East Parade.

Plastirion (*private*), East Parade.

Westcote (*boarding*), Victoria Avenue : *R.* and *b.*, fr. 3/6.
Boarding terms: fr. 6/- per day ; fr. 42/- per week.

An advertisement for Rhyl hotels, 1938.

Palace Avenue, Rhyl, viewed from the corner of Wellington Road and looking down towards the sea, *c.* 1910. Many of the houses seen here, especially at the far end of the road, would have been guest houses.

F.H. Homan's barber shop on Wellington Road, Rhyl, *c.* 1910. The staff, and what looks like the local paper boy, pose for the photograph. In late Victorian times many men would go to the barber for a shave, especially while on holiday. Note the barber's pole, always red and white, over the door on the left. In early times hairdressers were known as surgeon barbers and the pole indicated this, red signifying blood and the white wrapped round it the bandage.

Water Street at the side of Rhyl town hall, *c.* 1880. The large building on the left is the Congregational church (Christchurch).

Wellington Hall, owned by J. Beech, in Wellington Road, *c.* 1893. Wellington Road, named after the Duke of Wellington, runs north to south behind the promenade and sea front. J. Beech sold souvenirs and mementoes to visitors.

The children's paddling pool and Rhyl pavilion behind it, late 1950s. Rhyl was the perfect holiday destination for thousand of families as it had something for everyone – and there are plenty of happy families enjoying the wide promenade an paddling pool here.

A composite postcard of Rhyl, early 1960s. The children's cycle track, the roller-skating rink and the paddling pool made an exciting holiday destination for youngsters.

The church and clock tower at [To]wyn, just south of Rhyl, [in] 1959. In the years before the [S]econd World War Towyn was [ju]st the centre of a farming [c]ommunity and it was not [u]ntil the advent of caravan [p]arks that Towyn started to [gr]ow and was mentioned in [h]oliday guide books. [U]nfortunately, in 1990 Towyn [m]ade the headlines when the [se]a wall was breached here [an]d the whole area was under [w]ater for weeks. Thousands of [po]unds were spent repairing [an]d rebuilding this very [po]pular holiday centre. Today, [w]ith pony racing and a [w]eekend market, Towyn is a [v]ery busy place. The caravan [p]arks attract thousands to the [ar]ea all through the summer, [an]d this has been the case for [fif]ty years.

[A] postcard of Towyn's parish church, St Mary's, 1910. It was quite usual for people on holiday to go to the nearest local [ch]urch on a Sunday while they were away, and they would often send a postcard of that church to friends back home.

For "THE SIMPLE LIFE"

AT

THE WHITE HOUSE BY THE SEA

Ideally situated on Sand Dunes. Adjoining new Ffrith Bathing Beach and Golf Links. Supreme Sea and Sun Bathing.

Fully Furnished

Private Drive on to main coast road 5 minutes from Prestatyn 10 minutes from Rhyl. Frequent Bus Service.

FLATS
BUNGALOWS
LOG CABINS

SELECT CAMPING GROUND

FREE CAR PARK. ❖ ❖ STORE ON GROUNDS.

Send 1½d stamp for illustrated booklet to :—

Mrs and Miss MORRIS, The White House, Rhyl Coast Rd. Prestatyn, N. Wales. *Tel. Prestatyn* **289**

An early advertisement promoting the idea of holiday homes and camping, late 1930s.

The stony beach at Pensarn, *c.* 1900. The railway station can be clearly seen on the far right in the background – the station was the scene of a great tragedy in 1868. This is another area where the sea walls have been raised and strengthened to keep out the ever rising tides. Note the ladies in their Welsh hats, probably worn just for the camera.

Colwyn Bay &
Rhos-on-Sea

The pier and pavilion at Colwyn Bay, late 1950s. This is the third pavilion to be built on this pier and it remains today, although its future does not look very bright.

Looking up Station Road, Colwyn Bay, *c.* 1912. The shop on the right-hand corner is now the Colwyn Bay Information Centre and the street is host to an open-air market every Thursday and Saturday. The River Colwyn gives its name to the area. Some historians believe the word Colwyn derives from 'Can' meaning a hollow and 'Ilwyn' a grove. There is however a very old tradition that the word Colwyn was associated with dogs, and some old books refer to the Colwyn as a 'Puppy River'.

Station Road, Colwyn Bay, *c.* 1925. This was the main street of the new and growing Colwyn Bay. Today, it is a pedestrianised area and the local market is held here down the centre of the road.

he Victoria Pier and beach at Colwyn Bay between the two world wars. The pier was built in the 1890s but has been
lagued by fires for the whole of its existence. The pavilion we see here was the second one, opened in 1923 after the
riginal one was burnt down.

he Arcade and Catlin's Theatre, early 1900s. The large railway embankment at Colwyn Bay provided a chance to build
alks and parades near the beach. The theatre used to have a train timetable pinned up backstage so that the show could be
opped while the London express train hurtled through the town. The pierrots are entertaining the crowd on the right.

The promenade at Colwyn Bay, 1910. It shows the railway embankment and how it towered over the front. The effect of blocking the town off from the beach was softened when it was laid out with flower beds, shrubs and walkways, making it a positive addition to the promenade.

The promenade and front at Colwyn Bay, c. 1910. This photograph shows the Victoria Pier and its pavilion in their original splendour. This pavilion was destroyed by fire in 1922 and replaced by a much smaller building. There was another fire in 1933 and the present pier building was constructed in 1934. This postcard also shows a large audience enjoying the minstrel show, which was performed regularly on the Promenade.

54

An advertisement for the
Rothesay Hotel.

COLWYN BAY
THE IDEAL HOLIDAY RESORT.
"ROTHESAY" PRIVATE HOTEL
ESTABLISHED 1896.
ALSO RESIDENTIAL WINTER HOTEL.
LISTED HOTEL (R.A. CLUB).

West Promenade. Facing Sea. Magnificent views. Noted for good table. Sanitary arrangements perfect. Further Enlargements, 1926 : whole block. Dining, Drawing, Writing Rooms ; Smoke Room ; Lounge ; Dancing and Recreation Room ; 80 Bedrooms. Electric Light. Visitors can bathe from the Hotel. Near 2 Golf Links. Coaching, Boating, Tennis Garage for 50 cars.

Telegrams—" **Kirkpatrick, Colwyn Bay.**" *Telephone*—**2417**

COLWYN BAY
GRESFORD.

A composite card showing the glories of Colwyn Bay in the late 1940s. Three of the four pictures around the central map show rural scenes and the peacefulness of the area, which was one of its great attractions. In 1895 the Colwyn Bay & Colwyn Urban District Council including Rhos-on-Sea was formed and they constructed the Promenade at the front and extended it to Llandrillo-y-Rhos. They built an electricity generating station on Ivy Street and took over the gas works. In 1934 Colwyn Bay became a borough and took in Kinmel Bay, Towyn and Abergele. In 1996 Colwyn Bay became part of Conwy County Borough Council.

This open-topped tram is making its way through Colwyn Bay out towards Rhos-on-Sea. 1940s. The tram company that ran from Colwyn Bay to Llandudno was definitely a boon to Colwyn Bay. Although they cluttered up some of the main streets, the trams were very popular with locals and holiday-makers. The early Belisha beacon crossing is a fascinating piece of 1940s history, and was the forerunner of the Pelican crossing, which came much later.

Looking down on Colwyn Bay from Bryn Euryn, *c.* 1946. The railway line cuts right through the centre of Colwyn Bay and swings inland towards Llandudno Junction with the pier in the distance. At the time of this photograph the trams were still running too. In 1939 many government departments had moved to this area and so it became an important centre. It was at about the time of this photograph that they started to return to the south.

A Llandudno & Colwyn Bay Electric Railway vehicle making its way down Conway Road, at the point where the street name changes to Abergele Road, Colwyn Bay, 1949. The tobacconist shop Marshall's is on the left and our tram has almost completed its journey from Llandudno via Rhos-on-Sea. The open area to the right is the lawn in front of St Paul's Church, the parish church of Colwyn Bay. At this time Colwyn Bay was a 'black spot' for traffic heading for Llandudno or Anglesey, and in the summer months during the 1950s it could take an hour or more to negotiate the main road that ran through upper Colwyn. You could by-pass Rhyl and Prestatyn, but there was no getting away from Colwyn Bay except on very minor roads. In the 1950s a popular booklet was the *Captains Guide to Wales*, which listed all the back roads to take to avoid the traffic jams.

The grand sweep of Colwyn Bay, 1950s. While Old Colwyn and Colwyn Bay were Welsh, Rhos-on-Sea seen here in the far distance was always very English.

Colwyn Bay pier and promenade, *c.* 1948. Cars were returning to the roads after the petrol rationing of the Second World War. The wooden jetty in front of the pier was for embarking and disembarking holiday-makers – boat trips around the bay were made at low tide.

A view of Colwyn Bay from the 1930s. You can clearly see the railway lines and the goods yard just beyond the station that has today become a shopping centre. You can also see the Victoria pier, set in a wide expanse of sand. The pier was designed by the firm of Magnells & Littlewood of Manchester, and the cast iron for its construction was supplied by the Widnes Foundry Company. The construction work was carried out by Messrs William Brown & Son of Salford.

The long and bustling promenade at Colwyn Bay, *c.* 1960. From Old Colwyn in the north to Rhos-on-Sea in the south, the promenade at Colwyn Bay extends for 3 miles, and is the longest in North Wales.

An open-topped tram (No. 14) picks up outside St Paul's Church, Abergele Road, Colwyn Bay, early 1950s. The trams were ideal for advertising the summer shows as you can see on this picture. Here the attraction is Catlin's Follies, who appeared at different theatres up and down the coast for almost a century.

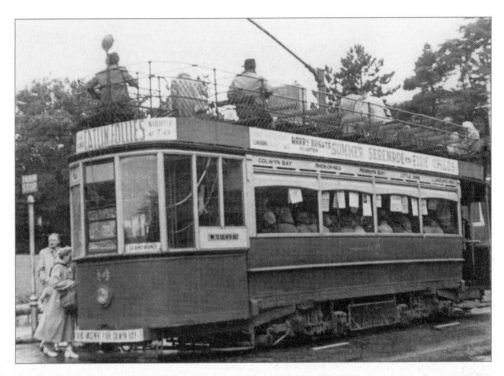

Rhos-on-Sea viewed from the air just after the Second World War. The Little Orme dominates the background and the pier can be seen bottom right. Colwyn Bay was the product of the growth of Colwyn and was a Welsh-speaking area and strongly attached to its roots. Rhos was conceived as being more English and somehow always has been. A long time ago monks from Chester and Aberconwy established a fishing weir at Rhos and English monks founded a church here. Llandrillo-y-Rhos may have been the old name for the settlement, but Rhos-on-Sea was always an English encampment on the Welsh coast.

An Edwardian view of Rhos-on-Sea showing the stony beach and part of the promenade. Although many thought of Rhos as just an extension of Colwyn Bay, it had its own identity and a different way of life to its larger sister. Rhos was a Methodist stronghold and had many temperance hotels where strong drink, or indeed any drink, was not tolerated. In fact it was said that Rhos had more temperance hotels than any other North Wales resort. There were many in the Methodist movement who looked forward to their week's holiday in 'dry' Rhos-on-Sea.

The front at Rhos-on-Sea, 1920s. The tram tracks and overhead lines of the Colwyn Bay–Llandudno trams dominate the quiet roadway. Rhos pier was purchased second-hand from the Isle of Man and floated over in 1895. It was demolished in 1954 – attempts to blow it up failed and it had to be cut up, bit by bit. Collectables, a colourful little shop, is where the old pier entrance used to be. It is open most days and is a delightful shop full of knick-knacks, old postcards and coins.

hos-on-Sea, late 1950s. At the time the
ashion was to include as many views as
ossible on a postcard. This one has seven
iews of Rhos on it, including (below) the
nce famous Rhos Abbey Hotel.

The Rhos Abbey was once a
leading hotel in Rhos. Even five
years ago it had an air of
Victorian elegance and old-
fashioned service. It was
demolished in 2001.

hos Road looking up from the
romenade, 1920s. Between the First
nd Second World Wars Rhos blossomed
s a temperance resort, while other
aces struggled to attract visitors. It had
one of the brashness of Rhyl, none of
e hauteur of Llandudno and its
odest, clean, healthy activities appealed
the more sober holiday-makers.

St Trillo's Chapel at Rhos-on-Sea. This is a reminder of the monks of Aberconwy Abbey who came down here to gather fish from the weir granted them by the Bishop of Chester. This 15 ft × 9 ft cell was faithfully restored in 1935 by William Horton, who had bought the Llandrylo-y-Rhos estate. Historians think that the walls of the present chapel could date from about 1500.

The Priory Hotel, mid-1940s. Rhos once had a real abbey and a priory. The abbey no longer exists and the priory is now a greatly modernised hostelry and makes a pleasant addition to the resort.

Llandudno &
The Great Orme

The front at Llandudno featured on a postcard printed in Bavaria, 1904. The name Llandudno comes from the 'holy place of St Tudno', which is located on the Great Orme where St Tudno's Church stands. Llandudno was manufactured out of the Victorians' need for a seaside resort, and was carefully planned and purpose-built to that end. This once out-of-the-way, boggy, useless area, bypassed by the main roads, was transformed into a thriving holiday destination.

The beach at Llandudno with the Pavilion Theatre and Grand Hotel next to it on the pier, *c.* 1900. Note the number of boats pulled up on the beach. Not only were trips around the bay and the head popular with the visitors but sea fishing and angling also added to the many attractions of the resort.

Happy Valley on the Great Orme at Llandudno, *c.* 1890. How simple our pleasures were then, and how nice to get fresh air and bracing sea breezes after the smoke of the Lancashire mill towns. Entertainers gather outside a tent to delight Victorian holiday-makers.

The pier, Llandudno, *c.* 1900. Ladies with their parasols are seen parading along the half-mile-long pier, mingling with the steamboat passengers, on a typical summer day at the turn of the nineteenth century. This long pier enabled steamboat passengers to land or embark irrespective of the tide, as well as giving good views of Llandudno and the mountains beyond.

An Edwardian photograph of a packed theatre in Happy Valley and Llandudno Pier. A holiday brochure from the early 1900s describes the area: 'Happy Valley is a wonderful addition to the amenities of Llandudno, especially for ladies who have children in their care.' The valley was given to the people by Lord Mostyn, lord of the manor, who owned the Great Orme and between 1900 and 1960 it proved a great boon to the town. One of the North Wales Steamships is about to call at the pier to take day-trippers back to Liverpool.

The Imperial Hotel, Llandudno, as featured in a 1907 brochure. A favourite with the rich and titled, it was one of the leading hotels in Llandudno.

The dining room of the Imperial Hotel, from the same Edwardian brochure.

An unusual view of Llandudno showing Mostyn Street from the bottom end looking into town, *c.* 1914. During the First World War many things carried on quite normally to begin with, and postcard printing and photography was not banned until about 1916. On the right W.H. Smiths boasts a circulating library and Trinity Church dominates the left of this postcard. There is only a single tram line running down the street at this time.

The Queen Victoria jubilee memorial that stands at the entrance to Happy Valley, 1913. This was erected in 1897 by Lady Augusta Mostyn (Lord Mostyn's mother) to honour Queen Victoria after sixty years on the throne. To the right of the photograph are the toll gates on Marine Drive. The 6-mile-long Marine Drive is a magnificent piece of road building and well worth travelling along as it takes you the long way round to the west shore.

Llandudno and the Great Orme are linked together and you cannot mention one without the other. The name Orme comes from the Scandinavian word for sea serpent; the headland appeared like a sea monster to the Viking raiders on their journeys up and down the coast. The area has been inhabited since Prehistoric times and copper has been extracted from deep within the Great Orme for thousands of years. The Romans came here to mine this copper and after they left mining continued until the mid-1800s. The headland became part of a signalling system to inform Liverpool merchants of the safe return of their vessels from all parts of the world.

An aerial view of the summit complex, *c.* 1930. At this time it was a fitness centre and golf club. Today, where the eighteenth green is marked here, is a pay and display car park. The Great Orme adds mystique and splendour to the area. and whether you ride up to the top on the cable car or walk up, you will be rewarded with some magnificent views.

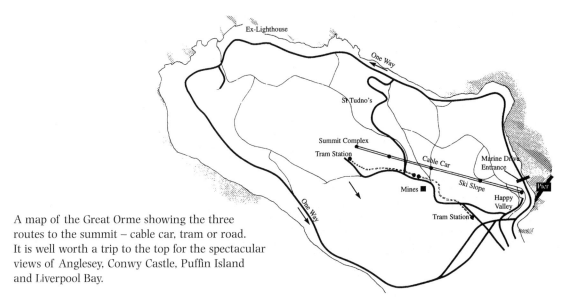

A map of the Great Orme showing the three routes to the summit – cable car, tram or road. It is well worth a trip to the top for the spectacular views of Anglesey, Conwy Castle, Puffin Island and Liverpool Bay.

St Tudno's Church on the Great Orme, Llandudno, *c.* 1922. St Tudno was a Celtic saint who preached Christianity in this area in about 550, long before St Augustine landed in England. He set up his cell on the Great Orme and many came to join him in prayer and solitude. Before Llandudno developed, St Tudno's was the parish church for the area. Once the town expanded and hotels and shops had been established, the growing population needed a more accessible church, so St George's was built in Church Walks and became Llandudno's parish church. This saved devout congregations from the long trek up to St Tudno's, though many members of the farming community still regard St Tudno's as their church. John Bright, the reformer, will always be connected with St Tudno's. He loved to walk the head, and his six-year-old daughter is buried here. In 1836 the roof of St Tudno's was blown off in a gale and the church was more or less abandoned for twenty years before its restoration. The townspeople were reluctant to pay for repairs on a church so far from the heart of the community.

A tram climbs the lower half of the tramway, which opened on 31 July 1902 The first section was 823 yards long, and the top half, opened a year later, was 850 yards. This picture dates from *c*. 1910.

The two sections of the tramway were separate, and transferring trams from the lower to the upper section was a job in itself.

Car no. 7 rests near the top in 1970.

The sender of this card depicting the Great Orme Tramway, posted on 11 August 1910, had been to Rhos that afternoon to see an aeroplane fly.

A tramway ticket for the Great Orme Chain Tramway from 1980.

The view from Deganwy Castle, *c.* 1950.

Llandudno's promenade and pier, *c.* 1955.

A superb view of the front at Llandudno, *c.* 1910. It shows a lovely tree-lined promenade, plenty of bathing huts (6*d* per person or 1*s* if more than one of the same sex or a married couple used them). In the distance sailing boats, the Grand Hotel and Pavilion Theatre can be seen, and overlooking all this is the Great Orme.

One of the single-deck trams on Mostyn Street, *c.* 1947. There was a wide variety of shops in Llandudno at this time, including H. Neville, chemist, the off-licence, the wine shop and the Oriental Stores.

'PHONE 6258   'PHONE 6258

LLANDUDNO
PIER AND PAVILION

THE CENTRE OF ATTRACTION AND ENTERTAINMENT IN NORTH WALES

THE FAMOUS **BROAD-CASTING SHOW**	THE **"FOL-DE-ROLS"**	IN THE **PAVILION** NIGHTLY at 8-0
HIGH-CLASS **ORCHESTRAL CONCERTS**	ALBERT **VOORSANGER** and the **PIER ORCHESTRA**	IN THE **PIER HEAD Music Pavilion** DAILY at 11-0 and 8-0
SEA EXCURSIONS	To MENAI BRIDGE BEAUMARIS, BANGOR THE ISLE OF MAN LIVERPOOL	FOR DETAILS SEE STEAMER Announcements
The FINEST **SUNDAY CONCERTS** in Great Britain	The World's Greatest Stars of Stage, Radio, Screen and Concert Hall	EVERY SUNDAY at 8-15

GET THE MAXIMUM BENEFIT OF THE **SUNSHINE AND SEA-AIR**

Buy a Weekly Ticket **2/6** as soon as you arrive

SPEND YOUR HOLIDAYS ON **LLANDUDNO'S FAMOUS PIER**

The Pier and Pavilion form the natural centre of entertainments and social life in Llandudno. You are invited to make them the centre of a healthy, happy holiday in the life-giving sea air.

This advertisement from the 1930s informs you that for half a crown you could buy a weekly ticket to walk the pier. The famous broadcasting team the 'Fol-de-Rols' were performing nightly at the Pavilion Theatre and Albert Voorsanger and his orchestra were playing to the crowds at the end of the pier.

Randolph Turpin, the world middle-weight boxing champion who stands out above all others in people's memories. He moved to the North Wales area when he was persuaded to use Gwych Castle as his training base in about 1950. Leslie Salts had taken over the castle and was developing it as an entertainment centre. Salts promised Randolph meals, use of the facilities and a bit of money if he used the castle to train and entertained the crowds as he did so. In 1950 he won all of his five fights and he was the nation's hero. Turpin and Salts purchased the Summit Complex for £10,000 at an auction in July 1952. Thousands flocked to watch Turpin spar in the outdoor ring they had built there. He was one of the greatest boxers of his time, but then Salts pulled out of the venture and Turpin was left to run it on his own. Unfortunately it seems that he was easily led and with false friends soon lost the fortune that he had made from boxing. The Inland Revenue were told to chase money he did not have and he gave up the Orme Hotel. His tragic end still did not stop devotees from making the trek up the Orme to the Summit Hotel and Randy's Bar, where his life is depicted in photographs and newspaper cuttings around the walls.

Church Walks in Llandudno, lined with hotels and guest houses, 1970s. At the top of this road you can just make out the Great Orme tram terminus. Before Lord Mostyn gave instructions to Owen Williams to create a great sea resort there had been plans to turn this area into a sea port, but the idea was not supported. Llandudno was purposely created as a resort for pleasure and relaxation and when wealthier people began to establish summer residences in the town it boosted the area even further. A finer, more genteel place could not be found and Llandudno soon became the ideal holiday destination. Even today it still attracts plenty of visitors, from home and abroad.

The wide 2-mile promenade at Llandudno, 1970s. A very long time ago this low-lying land was called Morfa Rhianedd o Ladies Marsh and consisted of little more than sandy hillocks, tufted with marram grass, the home of fishermen an seabirds. The Hon. Edward Mostyn, the greatest landowner in the parish, realised the potential of the area as a holida resort and instructed his surveyor, Owen Williams, to prepare and map out the new town. Plots went on sale in the summe of 1849 and were eagerly snapped up. And so Llandudno, as a seaside resort, was born.

A party of visitors and their guide, all wearing protective hats, about to enter the copper mines on the Great Orme, 199. There is a lot to see and do on the Great Orme and the ancient copper mines are well worth a visit. These mines are st being excavated and archaeologists hope to find more evidence of settlements, burial sites and smelting areas to give a tru impression of the people who lived and worked here and with whom they traded.

Conwy & Bangor

LMS *Mickey*, no. 45311, coming out of the tubular railway bridge over the River Clywd and passing Conwy Castle, 1958. The train stopped at every station to Bangor and did not go over to Anglesey. *(Locofotos)*

The waterside at Conwy, 1935. The River Conwy and the traffic on it was a very important part of the area. Deganwy can be seen over on the far side of the water.

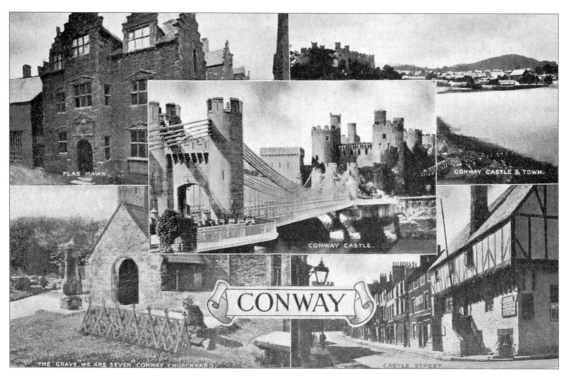

A multi-view of Conwy, 1930s. It shows the fine Elizabethan house Plas Mawr, a view of Conwy and the castle, the graveyard in St Mary's Church and the grave, protected by an iron screen, said to be that of a child associated with Wordsworth's 'We are Seven', a view of Castle Street and the suspension bridge and castle.

A late 1920s postcard of Conway (the English spelling); note the town and Welsh badges featured here.

Conwy Castle, mid-1990s. This beautiful area is a World Heritage site and should not be missed by any visitor to North Wales. Oliver Cromwell ordered that the castle be taken down so that it could not be defended and gaps were created in the walls, but fortunately, as can be seen here, many of the original towers were left in place.

A slightly unusual view of Conwy and the river. The photographer was looking from Deganwy across the wide mouth of the river. Traffic still had to go over the old suspension bridge and suffer hours of delay at weekends in the summer.

As well as its other attractions, Conwy boasts the smallest house in Great Britain. It is on the quay just past the aquarium and next to the Liverpool Arms, and is really just a gap between two houses filled in as a one-up and one-down for a local fisherman. When I was a teenager it was 6d to go in and climb the ladder nailed to the wall.

CONWAY COLLEGE,

CONWAY.

◆

High=Class Boarding School for Boys.

Picturesque and Historical surroundings outside and bounded by Old Town Wall and Battlements. On high ground, with splendid view of Old Castle and Gyffin Valley. Mountain and sea air. Good sea bathing. Near river Conway, affording safe fishing. Splendid cricket. Near to Carnarvonshire Golf Links.

FEES, 45 TO 60 GUINEAS.

THOMAS C. E. DANIELS, M.A., Head Master.

An advertisement for a boarding school, 1900. The Welsh coastal air was thought to be so good for people that many boarding schools sprang up along the coast.

Bangor Cathedral, *c.* 1920. This simple, low-lying edifice belies its long and colourful history. Founded in about 525 by Deiniol, son of the Abbot of 'Bangor under the Wood', as it was then called, the cathedral has had a varied history which has seen it destroyed and rebuilt. This is how it appears today, a rebuild by Sir Gilbert G. Scott. Although there are not many monuments inside, there are the graves of some Welsh princes.

Bangor pier, stretching out across the Menai Strait towards Anglesey, 1920s. At this time admission was 1*d*. The local joke was that if the pier builders had kept going a bit longer they would have made a useful footbridge to Beaumaris. The pier is officially called Garth Pier and was originally 1,550 ft long. It is still standing today, though it is shorter than it once was.

Summer Holidays

A charabanc from White Rose Motors, Rhyl, full of some early holiday-makers taking a trip, *c.* 1923. In Victorian times the rich and the landed gentry would go on European tours, but the newly emerging middle class preferred to take their holidays nearer home. North Wales, being a place of great natural beauty, attracted thousands of tourists. People wanted to get away from the daily grind but not everyone could afford an hotel. Boarding houses sprang up everywhere – establishments where people could stay but had to shop for their own food which the landlady would cook and they would pay a 'cruet' charge of 6*d* a week.

A general view of Gronant, 1946. What a mixture of resting places is seen here. There was even a flat-backed truck with tent pitched on the back at the camp for many years. The American concept of the 'drug store', is interesting, though today it would have a whole new meaning.

The sands at Gronant on a hand-coloured postcard, 1946. Talacre and Gronant are the first sandy beaches that you encounter in North Wales and have for many years been very popular with people from the northern cities of Manchester and Liverpool. There must be a million caravans between Talacre and Llandudno and while many are let out commercially others are second homes to hard-working individuals from the north-west of England.

The caravan parks at Gronant, revealing the mixed collection of holiday homes they contained in 1946. I was once told the story of a Liverpool bus driver who during the May blitz of 1940 had a bomb drop in front of his bus, but it did not explode. So, he went home and got his whole family, grandmas and all, and drove the bus to North Wales. The Liverpool Corporation had him listed as a war casualty and wrote the vehicle off. Locals remember a Liverpool Corporation bus being used as a holiday home at Talacre during the 1940s.

A quaint and charming Edwardian postcard from North Wales. The sending of postcards was an important part of the holiday. Today postcard senders often beat their cards back home, but in the first half of the twentieth century some people would spend an hour a day while on holiday sending and receiving postcards. Yes, it was popular to write to people on holiday or answer a card that you received on Monday or Tuesday, knowing that they would get your letter the next day.

Two advertisements from a late 1920s brochure promoting the North Wales coast. Just imagine a holiday home for £260 and, as the advertisement says, you let it for just two months and that is the year's mortgage paid. On the right we have an advertisement for a holiday in Kinmel Bay for just £2 2s a week. Included in that price are four meals a day, all charges and entertainments.

BRITAIN'S BRIGHTEST
£2-2-0 A WEEK HOLIDAY

- FOUR FULL MEALS DAILY
- YOUR OWN SEASIDE CHALET
- HEALTHY NORTH WALES COAST

SUNNYVALE HOLIDAY CHALETS
OPEN MAY TO SEPTEMBER

Corner of Main Dining Hall, with view of Chalets beyond

Charming location on North Wales Coast, near Rhyl. Mountains, Rivers, Golden Sandy Beach, and—the Sea ! A completely furnished Seaside Chalet of your own from

TWO GUINEAS WEEKLY

inclusive of FOUR FULL MEALS DAILY. Electric Light. Hot Water. Shower Baths. Central Dining Hall with separate tables for four. Dances. Cabarets. Tennis. Bathing. Boating. Fishing. Garage. Near Golf Course.

THE BEST BUILT AND EQUIPPED CHALETS IN BRITAIN

Illustrated brochure sent free on request. Write to D. Healey

SUNNYVALE HOLIDAY CHALETS
KINMEL BAY, VIA RHYL, NORTH WALES
Members of National Federation of Permanent Holiday Camps

Multi-view postcards came into fashion at the end of the Edwardian era. Maybe it was thought you got more for your money, or maybe people just wanted to show the folks back home just how nice their holiday destination was.

Railmotor No. 1 of the Dyserth–Prestatyn branch line at an open day, August 1905. This photograph was taken near the bay platform of Prestatyn station. Railmotors, with their engines under the carriage, were popular on many of the North Wales branch lines.

The waterfall and gardens at Dyserth, *c.* 1930. These falls were once thought to have healing properties and considerable numbers of people came here; it cost 6*d* per visitor. Today, the water still falls from the limestone rocks 40 ft up and it is still a place to see, though not by the same volume of people. This area is steeped in history, with the few fragmentary remains of Dyserth Castle on a rocky promontory about half a mile from the village, the Talargoch leadmines, which were worked from Roman times until the early twentieth century, and in a field near the ruined castle the remains of a fifteenth-century manor house of a shape and size common in many parts of Ireland, but rare in Wales.

A coach and horses waiting to take visitors on a day trip, *c.* 1900. The firm is Brookes Brothers of High Street, Rhyl, and among the trips offered on the boards outside we see Holywell and Pantasaph, a 45-mile loop tour and Llanerch.

A typical Crosville bus that travelled the North Wales coast, bringing and fetching holiday-makers and locals alike, early 1930s. It was during this period that Crosville took over many of the local bus companies and expanded their empire along the coast.

The marble church and the original A55 main Chester–Conwy road, just after the end of the Second World War. In the 1920s it used to take 6 hours to get to Llandudno from Manchester. Today we have the A55 dual carriageway that whisks the traffic past this spot, and on to Abergele, Colwyn Bay, Llandudno and all points to Anglesey.

n advertisement for one of the
ading Llandudno hotels at the
urn of the nineteenth century.
he staff of Vincent's Hotel line
p for the photograph, and look
ow many of them there are.
rivate sitting rooms facing the
ea and lofty and well-arranged
moking and billiard rooms were
ne selling points for the hotel.

VINCENT'S
High=class Private and Family Hotel,
... Llandudno.

❊

SITUATED in the centre of the **Marine Parade**,
and possesses the most extensive sea frontage on
the Parade ; also an uninterrupted and commanding
view of the Carnarvonshire Mountains.

Private Sitting Rooms facing the Sea.

LOFTY AND WELL-ARRANGED SMOKING AND BILLIARD ROOMS.

EXTENSIVE TENNIS COURTS.

*TARIFF (graduated according to the season of the year) ...
application to*

JOHN VINCENT, Proprietor.

enmaenmawr Mountain and Llanfairfechan, *c.* 1930. Though much smaller than the resorts, the village of Llanfairfechan
ttracted visitors who appreciated a quiet restful holiday. All the houses seen here probably took in boarders. The view from
ne front bedrooms would be across to Anglesey and Puffin Island.

The early horse-drawn coaches were all given names to make them sound grander. Steam trains adopted the same principle. In this 1900 advertisement 'The Prince of Wales' and 'The Wonder' are among Mr Hartley's coaches. As can be seen, quite a number of people could be accommodated: lovely on a fine day!

Coach Tours in North Wales.

TO VISITORS AND OTHERS.

MR. C. A. HARTLEY'S COACHES,

"The Prince of Wales," "The Old Times," "The Wonder," and "The Empress," RUN DAILY (and several times a day on the short routes), to the most

Picturesque and Beautiful Parts of North Wales.

For Fares and Times of Starting, apply at the Booking Office,

QUEEN'S HOTEL GARDENS, Clonmel Street, LLANDUDNO.

An open-top, single-deck bus at Rhyl, 1946. These enabled tourists to travel up and down the long promenade in comfort, while enjoying the air and the views. These buses were used mainly to bring in caravanners from the camps around the outskirts of Rhyl and were taken off the roads in the winter. Today the parks stay open for most months of the year, except January.

Trains & Boats,
Buses & Trams

A single-deck tram (No. 4) seen here entering the passing loop on Gloddaeth Avenue after leaving the West Shore Terminus, Llandudno. This photograph was taken just a few years before the tramway closed in March 1956.

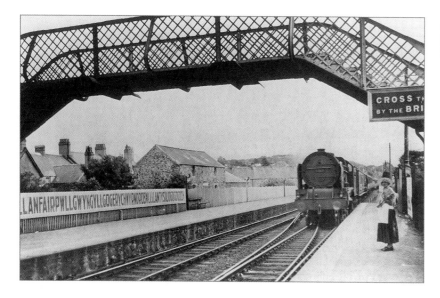

An original un-rebuilt 'Royal Scot' clas[s] passing through Llanfair PG with a lad[y] in Welsh costume on the platform, earl[y] 1930s.

LMS 'Black 5' No. 45089 is struggling a little with her heavy train approaching Llandudno Junction, 12 August 1961. In the years between the First and Second World Wars 20,000 people would be conveyed to the holiday resorts each week during the summer. Today we see trains of eight or nine coaches but years ago there would have been fourteen or fifteen packed coaches and they would stop at every resort. *(Locofotos)*

No. 41119 on the viaduct at Colwyn Bay with a stopping train from Llandudno to Chester, 1948. The line from Chester to Holyhead was the first great commercial incursion into the area and the Chester to Holyhead Railway Company was formed for this purpose in 1844. The railway line along the North Wales coast opene[d] in 1846 and the coastal resorts developed quickly after that. *(Locofotos)*

MS Pacific No. 46200 *The Princess Royal* at Llandudno Junction shed, July 1962. The North Wales coast line was usually erved by 'Jubilees', 'Scots' and 'Patriot' class locomotives. The big heavy semis ('Coronation' class) were not suited to this ne. The one exception to the rule in the 1960s and right up to the end of the steam era, was the 'Irish Mail' train, which ould usually have been pulled by a 'Britannia' class locomotive. *(Locofotos)*

MS 'Patriot' class No. 45537 *Private E. Sykes VC* pulls on to the North Wales coast line just west of Chester, late 1950s. At his time the trains were still long, heavy and full of passengers. *(Locofotos)*

No. 41320 in charge at Rhyl station at the 'down' platform, 1952. 'The Welsh Dragon' was the name given to this train, the Saturday and Sunday midday stopper from Chester to Llandudno. It had its own nameplate as this photograph shows, but was a push-and-pull working in the 1950s and early 1960s and was later replaced by a diesel unit. Below we see it working the other way and being controlled from the guard's end of the train. No. 41320 is on the other end of the coaches and still providing the power but the driver is really in the guard's van. *(Locofotos)*

Royal Scot' class No. 46106 *Gordon Highlander* has just crossed over from Anglesey to the North Wales coast, August 1954. The engine still has its original straight smoke deflects and unusually an excursion board (W378) on its smokebox. There were quite a few named expresses that came down the North Wales coast line, and the most famous of them all was the Irish Mail'. *(Locofotos)*

The Welshman' leaving the Menai tubular bridge in charge of No. 44986, 12 August 1960. The trains were long and heavy but luckily there were few gradients on the North Wales line. This train will stop at Llandudno Junction, Rhyl and Chester and carry on to London. *(Locofotos)*

Mostyn station at the turn of the nineteenth century. This rare photograph demonstrates how extensive and how busy the North Wales line was a century ago. Here we see the main line for through expresses, two other railway lines for the stopping local trains and two further lines on the right for the freight working along the coast.

A Whistler '40s' class pulls on to the fast line after stopping at Rhyl station, 1980. Diesels replaced the steam engines and HSTs replaced some of the diesels but the North Wales line is still one of major importance.

An LMS 'Black 5' waits at Llandudno Junction on a preservation special, July 1999. Because the line was never electrified it s ideal for running the old steam trains. The fact that there is a steam centre at Crewe only adds to the availability of these iants of the steam age.

'47' class diesel pulls eleven coaches towards Pensarn station, 1980s. Gwrych Castle can be seen in the background. J. Davenport)

Crosville's 'Sea Front Service' (146) passing the Palace Hotel, Rhyl, early 1960s. During the summer season Crosville ra▮ numerous open-top buses. This bus has been painted white instead of the usual Crosville green.

A Crosville double-decker bus on Abergele Road, Colwyn Bay, *c.* 1953, St Paul's Church is seen behind. The 408 service fro▮ Llandudno to Penmaen Head via Colwyn Bay and Rhos-on-Sea started in 1931. As the country recovered from the Secon▮ World War and traffic returned to the roads, it became more difficult to keep to timetables. This was especially so durin▮ summer weekends and bank holidays, and relief buses were introduced to maintain the service.

The 'Sea Front Service' passing the Woolworth's building on Rhyl promenade, early 1960s. This service was first introduced in the 1950s and started at Lyons Camp near Prestatyn and went on to Rhyl, Kinmel Bay and down to Winkup's Camp. It was the main transport for holiday-makers staying along the coast and even though occasionally passengers would have to rush downstairs to shelter from a shower, it was very popular.

Open-top bus XFM 223 on the sea front at Rhyl.

A coach from the Clynog & Trefor Motors waiting in Castle Square, Caernarfon, to load up with passengers for Pwllheli, mid-1950s.

Two trams pass in Church Road, Colwyn Bay, 26 August 1950. The trams had been very busy during the war years and were still a vital form of transport in the years that followed. It was not until the mid-1950s, when more people had motor cars, and the system was in need of a major injection of cash, that the Llandudno & Colwyn Bay Electric Railway ran into problems. The government inspectors said that some of the trams were too old and unsafe to run over the Little Orme and the track at Penrhyn Bay was in a very poor state. These were some of the factors that signalled the end of the line for the trams. *(H.B. Priestley)*

A single-deck, double-trolley on Mostyn street, Llandudno, tram (No. 6), *c.* 1919. The tram is passing the Carlton Hotel and approaching Palladium Corner.

Liverpool and North Wales
DAILY (SUNDAYS INCLUDED) SAILINGS

PICTURESQUE NORTH WALES
THE FAVOURITE ROUTE

LEAVES LIVERPOOL DAILY 10·45 a.m. arrives back 7·30 p.m.

FOR LLANDUDNO, BEAUMARIS, BANGOR & MENAI BRIDGE.

VIA LIVERPOOL AND STEAMERS
LA MARGUERITE, St. TUDNO, St. ELVIES, &c.

FREQUENT AFTERNOON SAILINGS.
Increased Services during June, July, August, and September.

Occasional Trips from LIVERPOOL and LLANDUDNO ROUND THE ISLE OF ANGLESEA, HOLYHEAD, &c.

Daily Excursions from LLANDUDNO to MENAI STRAITS and CARNARVON.

Frequent Trips ROUND THE ISLAND OF ANGLESEA, BLACKPOOL, HOLYHEAD, &c.

Splendid Sea Trips.—NORTH WALES & DOUGLAS (ISLE OF MAN) by Steamer "ST. ELVIES," one or two days each week. Three Hours Sea Passage.

Steamboat Connections between Rhyl, Colwyn Bay, and Llandudno for various Excursions.

Catering of Best Quality at Moderate Charges.

For all further particulars apply at any of the Pier Gates, or to
LIVERPOOL AND NORTH WALES STEAMSHIP COMPANY, 40 CHAPEL STREET, LIVERPOOL.
Telephone 5955 Central.   T. G. BREW, Secretary.

The front cover of a brochure advertising the Liverpool and North Wales Steamship Company, *c.* 1920.

St Trillo, one of the early North Wales coast paddle steamers, leaving Llandudno full of holiday-makers, *c.* 1910. Paddl steamers became a very popular attraction along the North Wales coast. Not only did they take tourists on jaunts aroun Anglesey, Puffin Island and even over to the Isle of Man, but they were also a ferry service. A service of sailing boats starte in the 1820s and sailed up and down the coast, but it was in the years between the two world wars that they were at thei peak. The service dwindled with the advent of the motor car. Originally *Trillo* was called the *Rhos Trevor* and run by th Colwyn Bay Steamship Company; she ran until 1921.

St Tudno of the Liverpool & North Wales Pleasure Steamers Co., 1947. This was the third ship to be named *St Tudno* and had begun sailing up and down this coast on 22 May 1926. In 1939 the *St Tudno* went into war service. The boat sailed fo the last time on Sunday 16 September 1962 and was laid up for the winter before being broken up.

lovely Edwardian view of passengers crowding on to a steamship at Llandudno. A sea voyage was one of the highlights of
North Wales holiday.

he *St Silio* in the Menai Strait, *c.* 1937. She joined the Liverpool & North Wales Pleasure Steamers Co. in May 1936.

The most popular of all the North Wales steamers, *La Marguerite*. She joined the fleet in 1903 and was known by the locals as Maggie. She had been built in 1894 and had been in service on the River Thames before moving to North Wales. Like many other coastal vessels she went to war in 1914 and with her captain, John Young, provided a great service. Her farewell voyage took place on 25 September 1925. Thousands turned out to say goodbye, and schoolchildren at Beaumaris and Bangor were even given the day off to see her for the last time.

La Marguerite at full steam coming round the head at Llandudno in the early 1920s.

Anglesey

The Britannia tubular railway bridge spanning the Menai Strait, 1920s. The bridge was designed by Robert Stephenson and its name is derived from a rock called Britannia Rock in the middle of the Menai Strait on which the central tower rested. *(Locofotos)*

The Britannia tubular railway bridge, 1975. In 1970 the bridge suffered a disastrous fire and as a consequence a study was undertaken to look at the problem of its repair and the increased road traffic crossing the Strait. The solution they came up with was unique and a compliment to Stephenson's earlier construction. It was found that the bridge was strong enough to take a road as well as a rail track, a tribute to Sir William Fairbairn of Manchester who built the original structure. These two unusual photographs show the repairs carried out in August 1975, with the stanchions extended and the tubes of the original bridge gone. The new roadway, which runs above the railway, was put on in sections just like the original bridge. Every effort was made to keep the railway line open during the three years of reconstruction work. (*Locofotos*)

enllech, one of the villages on the north shore of Anglesey, *c.* 1930.

his postcard showing Moelfre beach reveals a slower pace of life on Anglesey as recently as the 1960s.

> Church of St. Mary white hazel hollow ne:
>
> # LLANFAIRPWLLGWYNGYLLGOGERYCI
>
> The Record "Jaw

Llanfairpwllgwyngyllgogerychwyrndrobwll-llantysiliogogogoch

Church | Mary | a hollow | white | hazel | near to | the | rapid | whirlpool | Church | Saint's name | cave | red

A postcard giving the name Llanfair PG in full and explaining its meaning. There cannot be many places that are famous fc their name and nothing else, but this one on Anglesey is. Postcards with the name and platform tickets from the statio (nearly a foot long) have sold in their millions.

Above right we see the railway station with its now preserved platform sign. On the right is the Menai Strait and church o the island near Llanfair PG, from Anglesey.

whirlpool-Tysilio's Church of the red cave.

NDROBWLL-LLANTYSILIOGOGOGOCH

' with Translation.

Llanfairpwllgwyngyllgogerychwyrndrobwll-llantysiliogogogoch

Church | Mary | a hollow | white | hazel | near to | the | rapid | whirlpool | Church | Saint's name | cave | red

The mainland viewed from the railway bridge at Llanfair PG. On the skyline is the Marquis of Anglesey's column which was erected in honour of the 1st Marquis, who was second-in-command at Waterloo. On the very last day of fighting he injured his leg and it had to be amputated. He brought it back to North Wales and his leg was buried with full honours in its own small coffin in 1815. Thus Henry William Paget, Earl of Uxbridge, 1st Marquis of Anglesey, was present at the funeral of part of his own body. They put up the column two years after his triumph at Waterloo but did not add his statue until after his death at the age of eighty-five. He was then interred where his leg had rested. The column is on a rock 250 ft above the sea and is 91 ft high. Inside there are 115 steps to the top which commands magnificent views of the area.

HMS *Conway*, a naval training ship that was moored in the Menai Strait for about twelve years. She had been a battleship called the *Nile* but was given to a Liverpool charity and was anchored in the River Mersey off Wallasey in 1876. The Catholic Boys Reform Movement took youngsters who had been in trouble and turned them into seamen in the hope of giving them a useful life. Later she became a naval training ship. In 1941 when Liverpool was being pounded by German bombers the ship was moved to the relative peace of the Menai Strait and there she stayed, a colourful landmark, until 1953 when she went for a refit to the Cammell Laird yard at Birkenhead. Unfortunately she ran aground in the Strait and broke up before anything could be done.

A letter sent in March 1961 to a gentleman from Llandudno Junction who wanted his son to become a cadet at thirteen years of age. By now the original HMS *Conway* had gone and the training establishment had become shore-based. The *Conway* was not the first training ship in the Menai Strait as there had been one called the *Clio* anchored near Bangor pier from 1880 until 1920.

FROM CAPT. E. HEWITT, R.D., R.N.R. (RETD.)

THE H.M.S. CONWAY,
MERCHANT NAVY CADET SCHOOL.
LLANFAIRPWLL · ANGLESEY.
TEL. LLANFAIRPWLL 294.

9&837

EH/ILJ   2nd March, 1961.

D.C. Hardman, Esq.,
49 Maes Derw,
Llandudno Junction,
N. Wales.

Dear Sir,

I acknowledge receipt of your letter of the 28th and have much pleasure in enclosing herewith a copy of our prospectus wherein you will find most of the information you require, though there are two amendments to it. The basic fee is at present £285 per annum and cadets may join for a three year course in September as well as in January and May.

Although you state your son is already 13 you do not give me his exact date of birth so I do not know if he will be 13.9 when the next vacancies occur in September of this year but if so and you would like him to join then he will be required here for examination and interview on April 12th and 13th. A set of application forms can be found at the back of the prospectus. These should be in my possession if possible before the 15th of this month, if you wish your son to join us in September.

Before proceeding any further in this matter you should take your son to Liverpool for a Ministry of Transport Eyesight Test any Thursday or Friday morning and you are also advised to take him to an Opthalmic Surgeon to make sure there is no latent defect in his vision.

Yours faithfully,

119

Beaumaris viewed from the end of the pier. 1920s. Today as you turn off the main road and head past Plas Newydd to Newborough and Aberffraw you will find miles of golden sands, award-winning beaches, magnificent scenery and probably not another person. Go right as you come on to Anglesey and you come to Beaumaris and a string of charming fishing villages that have adapted to the tourist industry as fishing has declined. To the north of the island there are flat salt marshes that are a haven for migrating birds, and thousands of puffins and guillemots nest along the rocky coastline and in the RSPB sanctuary.

The view from Beaumaris across the Strait to the mountains of North Wales, 1930s.

Beaumaris Castle, 1930s. This was the last fortress Edward I built. It was started after the deaths of the Welsh princes Llywelyn and Dafydd in about 1282–3. It was built purely to guard the Menai Strait and was never captured. Completed in 1298, it had the most up-to-date fortifications and cost the grand sum of £7,000.

North Wales Today

There is still much of North Wales that is free and open to all. There may be an entry fee at Conwy Castle but Flint, Ewlowe and Denbigh Castle (most of the time) are free to visit. You can wander over the Great Orme and collect fossils from the Bishop's Quarry and no one will charge you a penny. Basingwerk Abbey is a beautiful, peaceful spot – feeding the ducks and birds on the water there is a joy for people of all ages. The new Sunday markets are a very important part of North Wales today but the coastal towns are bustling and friendly all through the week. There is history around every corner and always something new to explore in and along the North Wales coast.

The author with his granddaughter Hannah exploring the ruins of Basingwerk Abbey. The abbey is at the bottom of Greenfield Valley with Holywell situated at the top. Passing St Winifred's Well and travelling down the valley you come to an old inn, which was once a brewery, and the ruins of a paper-making factory. The water from the well is collected in reservoirs all the way down the valley and these were once used to power the factories there. Now they are a haven for wildlife. On the right is the overflow of one of the reservoirs that once powered a pin-making factory.

The ruins of Llys Eurn, situated in the hills behind Rhos-on-Sea. Although it is difficult to find and a considerable climb up to the hall, it is well worth the effort.

The North Wales Mountain Zoo. This attraction is set in some of the loveliest countryside in Great Britain and to see penguins waddle past and watch sea lions frolic in such peaceful surroundings only adds to the pleasure of a visit here.

The passenger ferry *The Duke of Lancaster*, which has been moored up behind the Abercan Mill at Mostyn for many years now. It does make people slow down and stare as they come down the A548 (the coast road), but its fate is just as uncertain now as it was ten years ago. It would be great if it could put out to sea again.

IN LOVING MEMORY OF
HENRY DAVIS POCHIN,
JUSTICE OF THE PEACE,
FOR THE COUNTIES OF LANCASTER, DENBIGH AND FLINT
DEPUTY LIEUTENANT OF THIS COUNTY
AND HIGH SHERIFF 1887,
MAYOR OF SALFORD 1866 AND 1867,
MEMBER OF PARLIAMENT FOR THE BOROUGH
OF STAFFORD 1868
WHO DIED AT BODNANT ON OCTOBER 28TH 1895,
IN THE 72ND YEAR OF HIS AGE
AND WAS LAID TO REST BENEATH THIS SPOT
BY HIS SORROWING FAMILY AND FRIENDS.

SLEEP SWEETLY, TENDER HEART, IN PEACE:
SLEEP, HOLY SPIRIT, BLESSED SOUL,
WHILE THE STARS BURN, THE MOON INCREASE,
AND THE GREAT AGES ONWARD ROLL.—
SLEEP TO THE END, TRUE SOUL AND SWEET.
TENNYSON.

The memorial to Henry Davis Pochin, who purchased the Nant estate in the early 1880s. He had already bought the spring at Ffynnon Asaph and the two mills, Grove Mill and Marian Mill, which were powered by the stream that eventually drops away at the famous Dyserth falls. In 1885 he bought the foreshore at Prestatyn from the ecclesiastical commissioners and set about transforming the small village. He had water brought in from Ffynnon Asaph and ran a pipe with taps right down the High Street. He built Bastion, Barkby and Beach Roads, Marine Drive and Bodnant Avenue, and he constructed a gas works at the top of High Street. He then went on to drain the Warren and create a foreshore complete with 'cobs', or embankments, with lock gates to keep out the sea water. Before this the Warren would flood at the high spring and autumn tides. He brought over windmills from Holland to pump out the water-logged land and made the foreshore suitable for development.

Acknowledgements

There are more people than usual to thank for helping to compile this book. Brian Hurst of Collectables at Rhos-on-Sea Point has been of great assistance and quickly answered all my queries and requests for bus and tram tickets. Andy Morley from Colwyn Bay Bookshop and the one at Rhos-on-Sea helped with some of the Victorian views. Ted Gerry, a postcard dealer from New Brighton, dug deep into his collection for me and as always Gordon Coltas, of Locofotos, willingly gave permission for the inclusion of his excellent photographs of steam trains in North Wales. I am grateful to Sue Morley from More Books at the top end of Mostyn Street, Llandudno, and Ron Jones from the Summit Complex and Randy's Bar on the Great Orme.

I have done my best to track down the copyright holders of all the pictures and apologise to anyone not credited.

The author aged seven exercising donkeys at Rhyl and carrying out some early research for this book.